How to Keep Slim,
Healthy and Young
with
Juice Fasting

How to Keep Slim, Healthy and Young with Juice Fasting

- REJUVENATING, REDUCING AND HEALING POWER OF JUICES
- FACTS, FADS AND FALLACIES ABOUT FASTING
- HOW TO FAST — AND HOW NOT TO
- WHY JUICE FASTING IS SUPERIOR TO WATER FASTING
- THE FASTEST AND SAFEST WAY TO REDUCE
- ACTUAL CASES OF RECOVERY FROM VARIOUS DISEASES THROUGH JUICE FASTING
- WHAT JUICES TO USE FOR SPECIFIC CONDITIONS

by **PAAVO O. AIROLA**, N.D., Ph. D.

HEALTH PLUS, Publishers
P.O. Box 1027, Sherwood, Oregon, 97140

Printed in the U.S.A.

TABLE OF CONTENTS

TABLE OF CONTENTS (Con't.)

How This Book Can Help You

There is much confusion and misunderstanding in the minds of health-seekers regarding fasting — **the oldest and the most effective healing method known to man.** Those who have tried to learn about fasting by reading books that treat this subject, are even more confused because most books contradict each other — some advise drinking pure natural water during fasting, some recommend the addition of juices, and some others, drinking only distilled water; some recommend taking enemas during fasting, others condemn enemas completely; some insist on staying in bed during fasting, the others advocate a normal working life with lots of exercise and walking, etc. There is also a great disagreement on the best method of breaking a fast. No wonder the average man, who is searching for the real truth, is confused!

This book is not a theoretical, philosophical work on fasting, but a practical do-it-yourself guide which will help you to understand the common-sense wisdom and mechanics of fasting, and help you to employ fasting for your own benefit — be it for prevention of disease and premature aging, or for treatment of the many ills of modern man.

I have studied various methods of fasting for several decades in several countries. My early teachers were two famous Swedish health pioneers Are Waerland and Ragnar Berg. I also studied fasting in Swedish clinics, especially those operated by Dr. Jern Hamberg and Dr. Lars-Eric Essen. Later, I visited the famous fasting clinics in Germany and studied modern fasting methods with such giants of biological healing as Dr. H.F. Buchinger, Jr., Professor Werner Zabel, and many others. Dr. Otto H.F. Buchinger, Jr., M.D., is, perhaps, the greatest authority on fasting in the world. Together with his father, also a doctor, he has experience with over 80,000 fasts which were directed and supervised in their clinics. Dr. Buchinger has the most modern and best equipped fasting clinic in the world, where thousands of patients fast under his supervision each year.

I have also had personal experienece with directing and supervising fasting of hundreds of patients and observing the results of various fasting methods on specific conditions. Some of these cases are described in the coming chapters.

In this book I will show you:
- The common misconceptions and fallacies about fasting.
- Why juice fasting is superior to the traditional water fasting.
- How fasting can be done in your own home; hour by hour instructions.
- Why juice fasting is the easiest and safest way to reduce.
- How water fasting without enema can be harmful.
- How juice fasting can rejuvenate your body and mind and make you look and feel much younger than your actual age.
- How fasting can restore health where other methods fail.
- What juices to use for specific conditions.

This is a small and concise book. The few hours it takes to read and study it may be the best and most profitably spent time of your life. Health is your most valuable possession. Vibrant health, youthful vitality, and freedom from diseases are worth working for. The application of the knowledge presented in this book can help you to achieve a better level of health and help to prevent premature aging.

Let me be your guide to a modern, scientific, health-restoring and rejuvenating miracle of juice fasting! Juice fasting not only accomplishes a physiological regeneration and revitalization of your body, but has a profound stimulating effect on your mind and mental facilities. It stimulates and sharpens mental and aesthetic perception and increases your spiritual awareness.

Let's make your juice fasting one of your most wonderful experiences, which will recharge, renew and rejuvenate your whole personality — body, mind and spirit!

CHAPTER I

Medical Science Rediscovers Fasting

Fasting is the oldest therapeutic method known to man. Even before the advent of the "medicine man" and the healing arts, man instinctively stopped eating when feeling ill and abstained from food until his health was restored. Or perhaps he learned this, the most efficient means of correcting any disease, from animals, which always fast when not feeling well. Certainly, nature provided man with a definite protective and health-restoring alarm signal, which suggests to him to abstain from eating by taking away his appetite for food.

Throughout the long medical history fasting has been regarded as one of the most dependable curative and rejuvenative measures. Hippocrates, "the Father of Medicine," prescribed it. So did Galen, Paracelsus, and all the other great physicians of old. Paracelsus called fasting "the greatest remedy; the physician within." Fasting was practiced by many great thinkers and philosophers, such as Plato and Socrates, to "attain mental and physical efficiency." Most Eastern philosophers and super-yogis, known for their long life, mental efficiency and spiritual awareness, fast regularly, along with meditation, to attain long life and a high level of spirituality.

With the advent of modern, drug-oriented medicine, fasting has fallen into disregard in the eyes of the orthodox practitioners. We are living in the age of "diets", when almost half of the population is constantly trying to "reduce" by way of countless restricted diets of every imaginable description. But the classic, and the best form of reducing — the total abstinence from food, or fasting — is seldom tried. Those who employ fasting, either for healing or reducing, are still looked upon as crackpots, quacks, and health-nuts, to say the least.

World-famous medical research center studies fasting

Happily all this has been rapidly changing. Doctors have stopped laughing and started investigating. Many scientific studies and clinical tests are being made, particularly in Europe, to determine the prophylactic, therapeutic, and rejuvenating properties of fasting. The Karolinska Institute in Stockholm, the world-famous medical research institution, has made clinical studies and experiments with fasting under the direction of Drs. P. Reizenstein and J. Kellberg. They employed fasts up to 55 days in their studies, which demonstrated that fasting is not only a perfectly safe measure, but that it also has a definite beneficial therapeutic property.

Famous Swedish fast marches

Perhaps the studies of the Karolinska Institute were inspired by the famous Swedish fast marches of 1954 and 1964 which are described in detail in my book HEALTH SECRETS FROM EUROPE (published by Parker Publishing Co., Inc., West Nyack, N. Y., 1970.) In these experimental fast marches, which made headlines in the world press, first 11 and then 19 men walked from Gothenburg to Stockholm, a distance of over 325 miles, in 10 days. Throughout each march the participants fasted — didn't eat any food at all! Dr. Lennart Edrén, D.D.S., who directed the fast marches, said after the 1954 march:

"This fast was the first in the series of experiments to

determine the effects of total fasting under severe conditions of stress. If we find out that fasting will not cause any damage to the body, but will, on the other hand, exert a beneficial revitalizing, cleansing and rejuvenating effect on bodily functions, it will supply invaluable information for healthy as well as for sick people. The healthy will be encouraged to fast in order to rejuvenate and increase vitality, and the sick to cure their ills. This experiment proved to the world the preventive and the therapeutic potentials of fasting."

Dr. Karl-Otto Aly, M.D., one of the leading biologically-oriented doctors in Sweden, and one of the participants of the fast marches, said:

"The march clearly showed that man can live for an extended period of time without food, even accomplish a hard physical effort while fasting . . . The general expressed feeling among participants was that they felt stronger and had more vigor and vitality after the fast than before it . . . The prime goal of these experiments was to stimulate scientific institutions to engage in a thorough and objective scientific study of fasting and its prophylactic and therapeutic potentials, so that fasting will be generally incorporated into the growing arsenal of medical practices for the benefit and blessing of a disease-ridden mankind."

Eminent doctors recommend fasting

Dr. Ragnar Berg, one of the greatest nutrition experts in the world and Nobel Prize Winner, said after the Swedish fasts of 1954 that the successful completion of this unprecedented fast was no surprise to him. He had fasted himself many times and also had supervised many fasts, including one of over one hundred days. He called the Swedish fast marches a "great scientific success."

Are Waerland is another great Swedish health pioneer who practiced and advocated fasting. Fasting is a standard initial cleansing method in the world-famous Waerland Healing System.

In Germany, there are hundreds of clinics, operated

by medical doctors, where fasting is now employed on a grand scale. For example, at the Buchinger Sanatorium in Bad Pyrmont, fasting is used initially in almost every condition of ill health. Well over 80,000 fasts were superviesd by Dr. Otto H. F. Buchinger, Jr., and his father, both medical doctors, during their 50 years of combined practice.

Another great fasting specialist in Germany is Dr. Werner Zabel. "Together with fever and optimal nutrition, fasting is man's oldest and best healing method," said Professor Zabel.

249 days on a juice fast

At the Stobhill General Hospital in Glasgow, Scotland, fasting was clinically tested with remarkable results. One 54-year-old woman with a painful arthritic condition and grossly overweight, was put on a liquid fast for 249 days and lost 74 of her 262 pounds. As a pleasant "side-effect", her arthritis cleared up completely, too!

CHAPTER 2

The Rejuvenating
Effect of Juice Fasting

The therapeutic effect of fasting is very well documented by actual clinical experience both in Europe and in the
United States. The records of the numerous American and
European fasting clinics prove the truthfulness of the state-
ment by Dr. Adolph Mayer, that "fasting is the most efficient means of correcting any disease." Fasting is, indeed,
in the words of Dr. Otto H. F. Buchinger, Jr., M.D., a
"Royal Road to Healing".

Fasting has been used throughout history, and is used
quite extensively now, not only for the therapeutic purpose
of healing disease, but also for its obvious rejuvenating and
revitalizing effect. Thousands of people throughout the
world fast regularly not to cure any particular disease, but
because they consider fasting to be an effective way to
cleanse the body from accumulated wastes, build up the
physical stamina and resistance against disease, and revitalize and rejuvenate the functions of all their vital organs. Particularly in Sweden, fasting has become a new
national sport. This is done in groups and individually,
mostly without medical supervision, but sometimes at the
numerous health spas. The objective of these fasts is a

periodic internal cleansing of the system and total rejuvenation of all the functions of the body.

Contrary to the poular notion, **you don't get weakened or depleted by fasting;** the opposite is true, particularly if you employ a juice fast. After juice fasting you will feel stronger and revitalized; your health condition will be markedly improved, your physical and mental working capacity greatly increased. You not only will feel revitalized but also will look younger than before fasting. And this is not only because of lost pounds, but mostly because the fasting has such a profound rejuvenating effect on the functions of all the vital organs, including the functions of the all-important endocrine glands, which are so decidedly responsible for how young or how old you feel and look.

The remarkable case of miss A. L.

I have supervised hundreds of fasts, and have fasted many times myself. I have seen many remarkable cases of the dramatic effect of fasting upon patients who were ill, as well as upon those who fasted primarily for the purpose of rejuvenating and revitalizing themselves. Here is one recent case to illustrate the point.

Miss A. L. came to our Spa in rather a desperate condition. She had been working most of her life in the field of health and beauty. She had operated a figure control salon in Los Angeles and helped countless women and men to better health and better figures through proper exercises, plus a gym type program of steambaths, swimming and work-outs. For years she had been a wonderful advertisement for the effectiveness of her methods. When she reached 45 her health and her looks started to deteriorate. She began putting on weight and, inspite of her rigid program of exercises, didn't seem to be able to control it.

The signs of premature aging appeared suddenly. Her hair started to turn gray. Wrinkles appeared on her face. In addition, she felt stiffness and pain in her fingers, elbows and shoulders, which was diagnosed by her doctor as early symptoms of rheumatoid arthritis. Also, her complexion began to deteriorate rapidly. Her skin was dry and lifeless, and patches of psoriasis appeared behind her ears. She felt exhausted most of the time and lost interest in her work. She sold her business and tried to find new interests — without success.

In the meantime she developed an uncontrollable appetite and was putting on pounds each week. She had always wanted work with young people and tried to get a job as a health, beauty and personality counselor in a home for young girls, but was turned down because of her "age and overweight". This incident was a great shock to her and a turning point in her life. She suddenly realized that she had to do something, and do it fast, if she didn't want to live the rest of her life in her words "as a fat, old, sick blob."

She had noticed with a horror that people started to feel sorry for her and that some of her former friends started to avoid her. Her personality had changed. Her outlook on life was negative. She had grown critical of everyone and everything, and her temper was getting worse and worse. No wonder her circle of friends was diminishing.

There are hundreds of thousands of women who are in a similar situation. They blame their "condition" on the "change of life" and usually become resigned to the idea that they are becoming old and that nothing can be done about it. But Miss L. was not ready to give up. She decided to pull herself out of her dismal condition. Although working most of her life in a figure control and beauty field, she never thought much about nutrition and what role it plays in health. However, when some friends showed her my books and the advertisement for our health spa, she decided to make a visit and give it a try.

Miss L. was 54 when she came under my care, weighed 184 lbs. and looked like 60. She told me frankly that she didn't care much about arthritis or psoriasis, but that she had to improve her looks and figure in order to "get that job" they had refused her in Los Angeles. She was ready to do anything!

I outlined a three month program for Miss L. First, one month of fasting on juices. Then a controlled raw food diet with special vitamins and mineral supplements for four weeks. After that, two more weeks of fasting and two weeks of dieting. I promised that she would lose at least 50 pounds and look more like 40 than 60.

Miss L. followed my program religiously. She received two glasses of diluted fruit juice, two glasses of vegetable juice, one glass of vegetable broth, and 2 cups of herb tea each day. In addition, she could drink one glass of natural mineral water and any amount of plain water she wanted. She took long walks, up to 5 miles a day. She was advised to take enemas twice a day, morning and evening. For arthritis, she followed a special program of biological treatments with dry brush massage, hot and cold showers, special exercises, castor oil packs, and thermal baths. All symptoms of her arthritis disappeared completely by the end of the first 30-day fast. And she had lost 28 pounds.

She lost an additional 12 pounds during the 30 days of raw-food diet. She ate three meals of the most delicious raw vegetables and tropical fruits each day in addition to the regular juices. She also took lecithin, kelp, brewer's yeast and vitamins B, C, A, and E. During an additional two weeks of fasting Miss L. lost 12 more pounds. By the end of three months, she had a total weight loss of 52 pounds.

When she left the spa, Miss A. L. weighed 132 pounds. From size 20, she had reduced to size 12, and had to shop for some new clothes before she could return to Los Angeles. She could neither feel nor see any traces of arthritis whatsoever; and the psoriasis patches behind her ears had vanished, too.

But you should have seen the change in her looks and her personality! From being an old, tired, apathetic, discouraged and disillusioned woman three months earlier, Miss L. now looked like a young woman of 40, filled with energy and enthusiasm, full of exciting plans for the future, determined to "get that job" she had been refused. Her vitality and enthusiasm were limitless and the change in her appearance was nothing but miraculous.

When she first began fasting, she was worried that if

she lost all of that fat, her skin would be loser and flabbier, and she would look even more wrinkled. I assured her that with this kind of scientific Juice fasting and the intermittent diet of vital foods and vitamin supplements, in conjunction with special exercises and dry brush massage, her system would be supplied with all the elements necessary for the effective regeneration and revitalization of her glandular activity and skin activity. Her collagen*—the deterioration of which is mainly responsible for premature wrinkles — would be strengthened and its elasticity restored; her new-cell building and cell repair accelerated; her muscle tone improved; her complexion receive new life. She was amazed at the fact that although she had lost so much weight in such a short time, her skin **was** tighter than before, her wrinkles **were** less noticeable and her previously muddy and gray complexion **had** acquired a fresh, radiant look.

---

* Collagen — intercellular substance that holds cells together, even the cells of the skin.

CHAPTER 3

Why Juice Fasting Is the Number One Healer and Rejuvenator

As I suggested before, the main causes of disease and aging are to be found in the processes of cell metabolism and cell regeneration.

First, as the famous Canadian "stress doctor", Hans Selye, said, "Life, the biological chain that holds our parts together, is only as strong as the weakest vital link."* You are as young or as old as your smallest vital links — the cells. The aging begins when your normal process of cell regeneration and rebuilding slows down. **This slowdown is caused by the accumulation of waste products in the tissues which intereferes with the nourishment of the cells.**

Each cell of your body is a complete living entity with its own metabolism — it needs a constant supply of oxygen and sufficient nourishment in the form of all the known nu-

---

* Hans Selye, M.D., THE STRESS OF LIFE, McGraw-Hill Book Co., Inc., New York

tritive substances. When due to nutritional deficiencies, sluggish metabolism, sedentary life, overeating and consequery poor digestion and assimilation of food, lack of fresh air and sufficient exercise and rest, our cells are deprived of the nourishment they need, they start to degenerate and break down, the normal process of cell replacement and rebuilding slows down and your body starts to grow old, its resistance to diseases will diminish and various ills will start to appear. This may happen at any age. Sluggish metabolism, constipation, and consequent inefficient elimination, causes retention and accumulation of toxic wastes in the tissues which interefere with the nourishment of the cells, causing disease and premature aging.

Second, only about half of your cells are in the peak of development, vitality, and working condition. One fourth are usually in the process of development and growth and the other fourth in the process of dying and replacement. The healthy vital life-processes and perpetual youth are maintained when there is perfect balance in this process of cell break-down and replacement. If the cells are breaking down and dying at a faster rate than the new cells are built, the process of aging will begin to set in. Also, it is of vital importance that the aging and the dying cells are decomposed and eliminated from the system as efficiently as possible. Quick and effective elimination of dead cells stimulates the building and growth of new cells.

Here's where juice fasting comes in as the most effective way to restore your health and rejuvenate your body. During the juice fast the process of elimination of the dead and dying cells is speeded up, and the new-building of cells is accelerated and stimulated. At the same time the toxic waste products that interfere with the nourishment of the cells are effectively eliminated and the normal metabolic rate and cell oxygenation are restored.

How can the mere abstinence from food accomplish such remarkable results? Here's how:

1. During a prolonged fast (after the first three days), your body will live on its own substance. When it is deprived of the needed nutrition, particularly of the proteins

and fats, your body will burn and digest its own tissues by the process of **autolysis,** or self-digestion. But your body will not do it indiscriminately! In its wisdom — and here lies the secret of the extraordinary effectiveness of fasting as curative and rejuvenating therapy! — your body will first decompose and burn those cells and tissues which are diseased, damaged, aged or dead. In fasting, your body feeds itself on the most impure and inferior materials, such as dead cells and morbid accumulations, tumors, abcesses, damaged tissues, fat deposits, etc. Dr. Buchinger Sr., one of the greatest fasting authorities in the world, calls fasting — very pertinently — a "refuse disposal", a "burning of rubbish." These dead cells and inferior tissues are consumed and utilized **first.** The essential tissues and vital organs, the glands, the nervous system and the brain are **spared.**

2. During fasting, while the old cells and diseased tissues are decomposed and burned, the building of new, healthy cells is stimulated and speeded up. This may seem unbelievable, since no nourishment or only a limited amount of nourishment (during a juice fast) is supplied. But it is nevertheless a physiological fact. During the famous Swedish fast marches it was observed that the protein level of the blood (serum albumin reading) of fasting people remained **constant** and **normal** throughout the fasting period, **in spite of the fact that no protein was consumed.** The reason for this is that proteins in your body are in the so called **dynamic state;** that is, they are changed from one stage to another, being decomposed and resynthesized constantly and re-used for various needs within the body. Amino acids, the building blocks of proteins, are not wasted, but are released from the decomposed cells and used again in the new-building of young, vital cells. As you know, your cells are made mostly of proteins and the complete set of all the essential amino acids is needed for the effective building of cells. During fasting the proteins needed for the new cell buildings are resynthesized from the decomposed cells. Thus the body is using and re-using the same proteins and other nutrients over and

over where they are needed.

3. During a juice fast, the eliminative and cleansing capacity of the eliminative organs — lungs, liver, kidneys, and skin — is greatly increased, and masses of accumulated metabolic wastes and toxins are quickly expelled. For example, during fasting the concentration of toxins in the urine can be ten times higher than normal. This is due to the fact that the eliminative organs are relieved from the usual burden of digesting foods and eliminating the resultant wastes, and can concentrate on the cleansing of old accumulated wastes and toxins such as uric acid, purines, etc. from the tissues. This eliminative process is evidenced by the following typical symptoms of fasting: offensive breath, dark urine, continuous and generous discharge from the colon with enema, skin erruptions, excessive perspiration, catarrhal elimination of mucus, etc. Keep in mind that the activity of the human bowel system is not limited to the absorption of nutrients from the foods and the elimination of the undigestable food residues. Bowels are also one of your eliminative and detoxifying organs in a general sense: through the intestinal walls the toxins and metabolic wastes from the blood and tissues are discharged into the intestinal canal to be excreted from the body. This internal excretion is accelerated during fasting.

4. A juice fast affords a physiological rest to the digestive, assimilative and protective organs of the body. Fresh vegetables and fruit juices hardly require any digestion and are easily assimilated from the upper digestive tract without putting any burden on the digestive organs. After fasting, the digestion of food and the utilization of nutrients is greatly improved, and sluggishness and further waste retention is prevented. The rejuvenated cells are thus supplied with nutrients and oxygen more effectively.

5. Finally, the juice fast exerts a normalizing, stabilizing and rejuvenating effect on all the vital physiological, nervous and mental functions. The nervous system is rejuvenated; mental powers are improved; glandular chemistry and hormonal secretions are stimulated; biochemical and mineral balance in the tissues is normalized.

It is easy to see from the above why juice fasting is such an effecive health restoring and rejuvenating measure, in addition to being a safe and fast way to reduce.

CHAPTER 4

A Few Actual Cases
Of Sucessful Juice
Fasting

Here, in a nutshell, are just a few cases of fasts, chosen from hundreds of cases, that I supervised in Canada, Mexico and Europe, to illustrate the effectiveness, and the broad range of application, of this, **the most effecive healing method known to man.**

Mr. C. H., 72; arthritis in knees and spine, neuritis in legs, emphysema

When Mr. H. arrived at our spa, he used a cane and could walk only a few yards with great difficulty. He had had arthritis for 35 years and underwent cortisone treatment 10 years previously. Due to severe painful neuritis in his legs below the knees, his nights were often sleepless. Only heavy doses of codeine-containing drugs made sleep possible. Even the slightest exertion caused shortness of breath due to his emphysema. He could not benefit from our thermal mineral baths and sauna because they were located 400 yards down a steep hill.

The day we began the biololgical program with a two week juice fast, Mr. H. asked me:

"I sure wish I could get down to the hot river and the

baths. Do you think I will ever be able to do that?"

"In a month or so you'll be hopping like a goat around here, even down to the river," I promised him optimistically, concealing as well as I could my own doubts that such improvement could some so quickly, seeing how incapacitated he was.

In less than three weeks Mr. H. was walking without his cane and one day he reported to me triumphantly that he had walked to the baths and up the hill all by himself — without his cane! After two two-week fasts on juices, herb teas and vegetable broth, with an intermediate special arthritic diet* including vitamin and mineral supplements, plus special packs, hot and cold showers, dry brush massage and a series of special exercises, Mr. H. told me one day that he walked over two miles up and down the steep hills and along the river and "without any pain in his knees or shortness of breath!"

"It's great! I can't believe it," said Mr. H. gratefully.

Mr. W. K., 68; angina, chronic low back pain, high blood pressure

A typical American business executive, Mr. K. took two weeks off his busy schedule to come to our spa, demonstrating that he was, after all, not really "typical." The typical American businessman works himself up to his heart attack and premature death trying to make his first million, never permitting himself time for a holiday or a trip to a health spa.

Mr. K. had blood pressure of 160/90, severe angina pains in the chest and a shortness of breath. He also had an arthritic condition in the lumbar region of his spine and several large fatty tumors in his body, one the size of an egg in his right forearm.

After ten days of fasting on juices and vegetable broths and 4 days of breaking the fast on a raw vegetable and fruit diet, his blood pressure went down to 115/70; arthritic pain in the lower back almost completely disappeared

* Outlined in detail in my book THERE IS A CURE FOR ARTHRITIS, Parker Publishing Co., West Nyack, N.Y., 1968

("90% better," he told me); he could walk for miles each day without chest pain or breathing difficulties; and his fatty tumor on the right arm was reduced to the size of an almond. It would probably have disappeared completely if Mr. K. had had the opportunity to stay a couple of more weeks.

Mrs. A. J., 64; high blood pressure, irregular heart beat, chronic headaches

After seven days of juice fasting Mrs. J.'s blood pressure went from 160/100 to 135/80. Headaches disappeared as if by a miracle.

She continued on a special salt free diet of raw foods with lots of garlic, comfrey, and special vitamin supplements of E, C, and B-complex with B_{15}. Her heart functioning improved considerably, and the blood pressure remained normal when checked three weeks later.

Miss C. F., 28; asthma

Miss F. suffered from one of the most severe cases of asthma I have seen. She had been totally dependent on a heavy dosage of drugs for over 10 years.

I suggested a fast on diluted juices for a week, to be followed by a strictly raw food diet, with a teaspoonful of plain lemon juice before each meal, several comfrey leaves chewed raw, and several cloves of garlic each day.

After one week of fasting, Miss F. felt so much better that she actually begged me to let her continue another week. At the end of the second week she still didn't have any desire to quit the fasting.

"I feel so good, with much less frequent attacks, that I want to continue fasting for one more week," she said.

After 3 weeks of fasting she finally broke the fast and started with a special diet and vitamin supplements. She took 1,200 I. U. of E each day, 3,000 mg of vitamin C, and 50 mg. of B_{15}. In addition she received B-complex, brewer's yeast, mineral supplements, lecithin, kelp and whey. She also took special breathing exercises, dry brush massage, and hot and cold showers in the morning.

She left the Spa so much improved that her medication was reduced by two thirds (after 10 years of constant use). Her breathing was dramatically improved and her vitality and strength greatly increased. She could now walk long distances without any discomfort or shortness of breath.

Mrs. L. K., 64; chronic bronchitis, chronic tonsilitis, high blood pressure

Mrs. K. had blood pressure of 150/90. She was overweight and troubled by chronic colds and chronic bronchial catarrh for over 10 years, with cough and a voluminous discharge of mucus.

In two weeks of juice fasting, she reduced 12 pounds, her blood pressure went down to 128/78, and her chronic bronchitis and tonsilitis were completely cleared up — no cough, no mucus, no breathing discomfort.

Miss A. Y., 48; arthritis, overweight, psoriasis

Miss A. undertook a long fast of 28 days. She used vegetable broth morning and night, diluted vegetable juices at 1:00 and 6:00 P.M. and diluted fruit juices (no citrus) at 10:00 A.M. and 4:00 P.M. She took enemas twice a day, hot and cold showers, and dry brush massage. She walked and exercised every day.

As her fasting progressed, Miss A. became more and more enthusiastic about the anticipated results. Instead of becoming weaker, she felt stronger with each passing day. She started with short walks, because of arthritis in her knees, but gradually increased the distance, until she walked about 5 miles each day.

Her arthritis, both swelling and pain, completely disappeared after the first 2 weeks. Psoriasis patches decreased in size gradually and after 4 weeks of fasting were completely gone. She reduced 25 pounds and looked not only healthier, but also at least 10 years younger.

Fasting, vitality and sex

Those who have never tried fasting and are not familiar with the physiology of fasting, usually think that fasting will make them weak. The amazing fact about juice fasting, which shocks and pleasantly surprises practically all those who fast for the first time, is that fasting actually makes them stronger and increases their vitality. During the first few days of the fast, the patient feels hungry and somewhat weak, but after the third day, the hunger usually disappears, and vitality and strength begins to increase with every fasting day. We advise fasters to continue with their usual work, if they are fasting at home, or to do lots of exercise and walking if they are fasting under supervision at a spa. Our patients usually walk long distances, some as much as 5 to 10 miles a day. Walking in the open is the best and most beneficial form of exercise for any age or any condition, as well as the best way to prevent disease.

I have made a remarkable observation during many years of supervising fasts. Many men have reported that they have experienced a renewed sexual vigor after 7, 10 or more days of fasting.

One man, age 62, who felt his sexual life had been very inadequate for a long time, told me that on the 8th day of fasting he suddenly felt such a sex urge that he was not able to refrain from sexual intercourse. He was somewhat reluctant because he certainly didn't expect "this sort of thing" during the fast. His wife told him, "Darling, you should fast more often!"

Another striking case was that of Dr. N. D., who was 78 years old and fasted under my supervision for his arthritis. He told me after 6 days of fasting:

"A most extraordinary thing happened yesterday! I had a most wonderful sex affair with my wife. For the last 7 or 8 years, my sex life was rather sporadic; and in the last 6 months or so I had nothing but the sweet memories of the past. But yesterday . . . How can you explain that?"

I can explain "that". A life-long sexual virility is every man's birthright. "Bedroom fatigue" is not caused by old age, but by neglected, malnourished and atrophied endocrine glands, which are responsible for deteriorating physical and sexual vitality. Premature signs of aging, loss of interest in sex, bulging waistline — all these are signs of insufficiently functioning endocrine or sex glands and diminished sex hormone production. Fasting has an energizing, invigorating effect on the activity and functions of all organs and glands, including the functions of the endocrine gland. I have heard many reports of the rejuvenating and revitalizing effect of fasting on sexual vigor and ability.

Sex urge is motivated by extra, **surplus** energy. A sick man is a poor lover. All his energy goes on trying to keep going, fighting chronic fatigue and pain. The ill man has no surplus energy left for sex. Fasting restores health, normalizes all the body functions, wipes out pain and gives new vitality and energy surplus. The renewed sexual drive is one of the surest indications that health and strength have returned.

CHAPTER 5

Is Fasting Safe?

The actual cases cited earlier show how safe fasting is. Fasting up to 40 days on water and up to 100 days, or even longer, on juices, is considered perfectly safe. In the Swedish hospital experiments, patients fasted 55 days without any apparent harm. I know of a perfectly healthy young man of 27 who fasted 143 days; not for any particular disease, not even as an anti-Vietnam demonstration, but **to cleanse, regenerate and rejuvenate his body and mind.** One Scottish woman, mentioned before, fasted 249 days on juices and not only did she not harm herself, but she improved her looks and her health considerably. In European clinics thousands of patients have fasted up to 40 days. And the Swedish fast marches demonstrated very dramatically the safety of fasting, even during adverse conditions of severe stress.

The truth is that **fasting is one of the safest healing methods known to medical science.** As a matter of fact, you can live without food for months, but can kill yourself by overeating in a few weeks. During **involuntary,** prolonged starvation, the negative state of mind and fear for life exerts a paralyzing, disruptive and destructive effect on all body functions, and will cause both physical damage and eventual death. Only during **intentional** fasting, when you have complete understanding, confidence, and faith in the constructive, beneficial effect of fasting, will your body initiate its health-restoring and regenerative processes and receive nothing but a beneficial effect.

Naturally, if you suffer from a serious condition such as cancer, diabetes, tuberculosis, cardio-vascular disorder, or any other serious disease, you should be at all times under a doctor's supervision. Although juice fasting up to 10 days or two weeks, is not a dangerous measure and could be undertaken at home and without supervision, my advice is that if you do not have a thorough understanding and insight into all phases and details of fasting, you should try to find an experienced practitioner who will supervise your fast. This will give you peace of mind and confidence in the treatment, which are imperative for the successful outcome of any therapeutic measure. The cleansing and health-restoring activity of fasting will bring about many physiological changes in your body. These changes may manifest themselves in certain discomforts, or what is called fasting crisis, such as headache, coated tongue, foul breath, dizziness, skin eruptions, and, occasionally, even temporary worsening of the condition. When fasting is supervised by an experienced practitioner, he will assure you that these reactions should give you no cause for concern; they are common symptoms of fasting, and properly understood, should not discourage you from continuing with the fast.

What about fasting and DDT?

It has been suggested by some writers recently that because of the universal poisoning by DDT, fasting can be dangerous. DDT, to which we all are exposed these days through insecticide contaminated foods, is a cumulative poison which is stored in the fat tissues of the body. During fasting, when the body starts to feed itself on its own tissues, fat is broken down and digested, releasing dangerous amounts of DDT into the blood stream. This can cause symptoms of acute DDT poisoning.

The dangers of DDT poisoning during reducing regimes or fasting, due to the rapid breakdown of fat tissues, has been known for a long time. The way fasting is administered in some American clinics — a total water fast without enema and staying in bed — a sudden DDT release can be dangerous. When fasting is done correctly, however, the danger is minimal. If you fast according to the recommendations of this book on fresh fruit and vegetable juices and vegetable broth, plenty of exercise and daily enemas you are well protected from any real danger in this respect. **First,** DDT is released into the blood stream more slowly than in a total water fast; and **second,** DDT and other poisons are better neutralized and more efficiently and safely excreted from the body because of the rich mineral and vitamin content of the juices and broth, particularly the vitamin C, calcium and potassium. Daily enemas, the extensive program of revitalizing skin activity, lots of walking and deep breathing, and the medicinal, protective effect of raw fruits and vegetable juices, broths and herb teas — all these help to make your fasting perfectly safe, even in respect to the release of DDT into the bloodstream. It would be advisable, however, that if you are quite overweight, and want to fast strictly for reducing, you should go on a series of short fasts (one week or 10 days fasts) instead of one very long fast. This way the fat tissues will be burned at a slower rate, and toxins released at intervals and eliminated from your system more safely. Also, the addition of high doses of certain vitamins and food supplements, especially vitamin C, to the diet between fasts will help to protect your body from the harmful effects of toxic substances.

How long can you fast?

If fasting is undertaken for **prophylactic** purposes, that is, to cleanse, regenerate and rejuvenate the body, one week or 10 days of fasting will be sufficient. Such short fasts can be taken once or twice a year. The length of the **therapeutic** fast, or fast undertaken with the purpose of healing, should be determined by the doctor or practitioner, who supervises the fast. The length of therapeutic fasts varies between 7 days and 40 days. The most common length of fasts in European clinics is 14 to 21 days. It would not be advisable to undertake a do-it-yourself fasting program for longer than one week or ten days. If you have a proper mental attitude, confidence and understanding of the philosophy and physiology of fasting, you can safely fast on your own up to 10 days. Remember, you are not the first to try it — millions of people have done it successfully before you. I know you will be surprised and amazed both at the safety and the miraculous health-restoring and rejuvenating effect of fasting.

CHAPTER 6

Periodic Juice Fasting Can Keep You Slim, Healthy and Young

Earlier in the book you have read the remarkable story of Miss A. L., who stayed at our spa three months, fasted 44 days and lost a total of 52 pounds. From an old-looking, flabby, chronically tired and disillusioned woman, size 20, Miss L. has changed into a size 12, vibrant, enthusiastic woman who looked 20 years younger than her actual age, full of energy and youthful vitality.

But let me continue with the story of Miss A. L.

As you remember, Miss L., although she suffered from arthritis and psoriasis, came to our spa **primarily to reduce.** She was refused the job she wanted very badly — because of her obesity — and she was determined to "get that job back." When she left the spa, she had not only lost 52 pounds, but also got rid of arthritis in her hands and knees and of psoriasis patches behind her ears. She left with all the guests and the staff of the spa admiring her new figure and youthful looks and wishing her the best of success in the future.

One year had passed before I had the opportunity to see Miss L. again. She came to one of my lectures in Los Angeles and, to my pleasant surprise, I noticed that she looked better, slimmer, healthier and younger than when she left us. She told me, laughingly:

"No, I didn't get that job I so coveted. Actually, I didn't really want it anyway. I started my own business again — as a figure and beauty adviser — and I just enjoy it so!"

"I must tell you that you look great! How do you manage to keep so slim? I remember you had such a hard time staying away from the food", I asked.

"How?" she laughed. "You should know how — I just followed your advice. Remember: **periodic fasting!?** I fast one day each week and take a 2-week juice fast every two or three months. Of course, I try to follow your diet, too."

There are an estimated 80 million overweight people in the United States. Do you know that it is not cancer or heart disease that are our biggest killers — it is **obesity!** The obese people run a hundred per cent greater chance to contract the above mentioned diseases, as well as many other killing diseases.

There are countless reducing diets on the market. Most of them will take pounds off, but only by the high price of ruining your health. Some reducing diets are so unhealthful, so health-damaging that they cause weight loss by making you **sick!** High-protein meat or egg diets, for example, cause such a severe auto-toxemia, acidosis and metabolic and biochemical imbalance in the system that you begin to lose weight by getting sick and literally fading away; and if you continue on such a diet long enough it will eventually lead to serious diseases that may even kill you.

Let's face it, the only sensible and safe way to reduce is to eat less and to eat the health-promoting foods. Systematic undereating will not only keep you slim, but also will improve your health.

But, here is the crux: **Undereating** is the word that is easy to say but . . . oh, how difficult to practice! As many compulsive eaters will testify, eating less is more difficult than not eating at all! In my experience, it is much easier for most people to reduce weight by total fasting than by cutting down on the amount of food. Particularly juice fasting is the most suitable for purpose of reducing. It keeps hunger to a minimum while it takes inches and pounds off faster than any other reducing regime.

The fastest and safest way to reduce

The **number one** requirement for any reducing system must be: **is it 100% safe?** The reducing diet should not only be able to take pounds and inches off, but also be able to supply your body with the necessary nutrients to keep it in top health condition while and after you reduce. Juice fasting fills such a requirement.

Juice fasting is the fastest and safest way to reduce! On the average, you lose one pound a day. A 14-day fast will take off 14 pounds. If you follow the directions of juice fasting and breaking of the fast given in this book **very carefully,** you can undertake one or two week juice fasting on your own, right in your own home. And you can continue with all your regular activities while fasting. Follow the example of Miss L. and fast regularly one day each week and one or two weeks once in every two months. While most reducing diets can harm your health, the juice fasting not only will reduce you safely, but it may actually **improve** your health — while reducing — and make you feel and look younger.

CHAPTER 7

Why Juice Fasting Is Superior to Water Fasting

The classic form of fasting is a pure water fast — the abstinance from all foods or drinks with the exception of pure water. The renaissance of water fasting in the United States happened around the turn of the century. It was popularized here mainly by immigrant European nature-cure practitioners.

While in the last few decades the fasting methods in Europe have completely changed — and now practically all European clinics use exclusively juice fasting — most American practitioners and clinics specializing in fasting still use the antiquated water fast method. I have supervised both types of fasting and am thoroughly convinced of the superiority of juice fasting. Dr. Otto H. F. Buchinger, who has supervised more fasts than any other doctor (over 80,000 fasts), employs only juice fasting. He told me that, in his experience, fasting on the fresh raw juices of fruits and vegetables, plus vegetable broths and herb teas, results in much faster recovery from disease and more effective cleansing and rejuvenation of the tissues than does the traditional water fast.

The scientific justification of juice fasting

The scientific justification of juice fasting is based on the following physiological facts:

- Raw juices, as well as freshly made vegetable broths, are rich in vitamins, minerals, trace elements and enzymes.
- These vital elements are very easily assimilated directly into the bloodstream, without putting a strain on the digestive system — thus they do **not** disrupt the healing and rejuvenating process of autolysis, or self-digestion, as suggested by some water fast proponents.
- Contrary to the opinion of some writers, fruit and vegetable jujices do **not** stimulate the secretion of hydrochloric acid in the stomach, which can lead to ulcers. Hydrochloric acid is mainly secreted when protein-rich foods are eaten.
- The nutritive elements from the juices are extremely beneficial in normalizing all the body processes, supplying needed elements for the body's own healing activity and cell regeneration, and, thus, speeding the recovery.
- Raw juices and vegetable broths provide an alkaline surplus which is extremely important for the proper acid-alkaline balance in the blood and tissues, since blood and tissues contain large amounts of acids during fasting.
- Generous amounts of minerals in the juices, particularly in the vegetable broth, help to restore the biochemical and mineral balance in the tissues and cells. Mineral imbalance in the tissues is one of the main causes of diminished oxygenation, which leads to disease and the premature aging of cells.
- According to Dr. Ralph Bircher, raw juices contain an as yet unidentified factor which stimulates what he calls a micro-electric tension in the body and is responsible for the cells' ability to absorb nutrients from the blood stream and effectively excrete metabolic wastes.

Thus, raw juice fasting is of particular importance when you fast for the regeneration and the rejuvenation of your body. Juice fasting will help to break down and dispose of the old dying cells, revitalize the active cells, and accelerate the new-building of young, vital cells.

Here is what Dr. Ragnar Berg, perhaps the world's greatest authority on nutrition and biochemistry, said about the superiority of juice fasting to water fasting:

"During fasting the body burns up and excretes huge amounts of accumulated wastes. We can help this cleansing process by drinking alkaline juices instead of water while fasting. I have supervised many fasts and made extensive tests of fasting patients, and I am convinced that drinking alkaline-forming fruit and vegetable juices, instead of water, during fasting will increase the healing effect of fasting. Elimination of uric acid and other inorganic acids will be accelerated. And sugars in juices will strengthen the heart . . . Juice fasting is, therefore, the best form of fasting."

Are you fasting or not?

The proponents of water fast like to tell you that the juice fast is not a fast, it is a **liquid diet.** They misunderstand the therapeutic meaning of fasting. **Any condition when your body is encouraged to initiate the process of autolysis, or self-digestion, is fasting.** During juice fasting, when no solid foods, proteins or fats are consumed, your body will decompose and burn all the diseased and inferior protein and fat tissues, **just as it does during the water fast.** Juices are absorbed directly into the bloodstream without the usual process of digestion. The only difference between the juice fast and the water fast is that during the juice fast your body's eliminative and detoxifying capacity is increased; the healing processes are speeded up and you feel less debilitated. But if someone insists upon calling this superior healing, reducing and rejuvenating method a **juice diet,** instead of a **juice fast,** let him do it if it makes him happy!

CHAPTER 8

Should You Take Enemas and Colonics?

There is a great deal of controversy on the advisability of enemas during fasting. There are some practitioners in the United States who condemn the use of enemas or colonic irrigations completely. They claim that enemas are unnecessary, unnatural, harmful and habit-forming. Discussing the enema question, the "anti-enemists" love to retort with the argument, "Animals do not take enemas when they fast. Why should man?"

How could one respond to the above fatuous reasoning except by saying the animals do not write books, give health lectures or engage in medical research either! In all fairness, however, it must be said that "anti-enemists" are right in saying that enemas are unnatural and habit-forming. As a rule, enemas should not be used regularly or for prolonged periods, as, for example, a regular routine to cope with chronic constipation. The emptying of your bowel is accomplished "naturally" by regular muscle contractions in the intestines, called peristalsis. These contractions are started in healthy individuals by the special defecation-reflex which is triggered by pressure from the filled rectum. The enema fills the rectum with water, and causes an artificial, strong pressure that triggers the defecation mechanism. If used regularly, enemas, with their instant and powerful pressure, will weaken the natural sensitivity of the mechanism; after a while, it will not readily respond to the more subtle, natural stimulus. Therefore, those who make a daily habit of using enemas will find that their bowels have lost the natural ability to empty the wastes. Thus, enemas used regularly can be considered habit-forming.

However, the above reasoning has nothing to do with the **use of enemas during fasting.** While virtually all European fasting specialists warn against the regular use of enemas and colonics, they **all agree** that there are some **important exceptions to this rule.** The most notable of these is fasting. (The other conditions where an enema is advised are acute constipation and acute infectious diseases, and when the patient is bedridden for prolonged periods, which, because of total lack of motion, causes sluggishness in normal bowel movements.)

During fasting, the natural stimulation of the defecation-reflex from food is missing and therefore all the impurities, wastes and toxins will remain in the body and may cause autotoxemia, or self-poisoning. The main purpose of fasting is to help the body to cleanse itself from accumulated toxic wastes. By the process of autolysis, a huge amount of morbid matter, dead cells and diseased tissues are burned; and the toxic wastes which have accumulated in the tissues for years, causing disease and premature aging, are loosened and expelled from the system. The alimentary canal, the digestive and eliminative system, is the main road by which these toxins are thrown out of the body. Since, during fasting, the natural bowel movements cease to take place, the toxic wastes would have no way of leaving the system, except with the help of enemas and colonics. This is why virtually all biological doctors in Europe administer enemas to all fasting patients — once, twice and even three times a day. **Enemas during fasting will assist the body in its cleansing and detoxifying effort by washing out all the toxic wastes from the alimentary canal.**

Constipation is one of the most common ailments of civilized man. As a consequence of long-standing constipation, the digestive tract, particularly in the lower bowels and colon, becomes slack and stagnant with hardened residues clinging to the walls of the colon and filling its many pockets and folds. This results in putrefaction and gas, forming a source of slow poisoning of the whole body. Diverticulitis, a chronic condition where small pouches and pockets of the colon are packed with feces, is one of the most common complaints of most people over 50, particularly women. Often the whole length of the colon is completely packed with old, hardened fecal matter, cemented to the walls and pockets, leaving only a thin, narrow channel which enables soft feces to pass through. To let the patients fast without making an effort to wash out this constant source of auto-intoxication, is indeed unwise. During fasting, copious amounts of toxins are released from the tissues and thrown into the bloodstream for elimination. If these toxins can not come out through the alimentary canal, the body will try to get them out through other eliminative organs, particularly through the kidneys, which, as a result, **will often be overloaded and even damaged.**

At our Spa, all fasting patients are given daily enemas in addition to colonic irrigations once a week. To further assist the body in its detoxification and elimination processes, fasting patients are given dry brush massage twice a day to stimulate the eliminative capacity of the skin, the biggest eliminative organ. Patients are also advised to walk and exercise in fresh air as much as possible to help the lungs in their blood-purification work.

Fasting without enemas can be harmful

I have seen rather horrifying examples of what prolonged water fasting without enemas can do. A few months ago, a man arrived at our Spa from recent treatments at a famous American clinic where he fasted for 32 days on water. During all this time he was advised to stay in bed, with the exception of short periods of sunbathing. He was given no enemas or colonic irrigations. He told me that it took him two months "to recuperate" from this fast and get on his feet. He was still in a very weak condition with damaged kidneys and severe edema in his legs. Several former patients of this particular clinic advised me that they were told at the clinic that it takes an amount of time equal to the fasting time to recuperate from the effects of fasting. That is, one month of fasting will require one month of recuperating. When this man told me of his experience, I showed him one of our enema-taking patients, who was just completing the last day of his one-month juice fast. He was active all the time during fasting, walked 3 to 5 miles each day, took yoga and other exercises, **had enemas twice a day**, and felt on the last day of the fast stronger and healthier than before the fast. He was actually loaded with vitality. This patient did not need any recuperating period after his fast — **his fast indeed WAS a recuperative and regenerative period!**

Of course, fasting is such a miraculous healing measure that even fasting on water and **without** enemas accomplishes some good. But how much better results the fasting would accomplish **with** enemas and the addition of raw juices!

How to take an enema

To take an enema, you must have an enema can or bag with a rubber hose and a nozzle; it can be obtained at any drug store.

Fill the enema bag with lukewarm water, about 99 degrees F. Add a few drops of fresh lemon juice, or a cup of camomile tea (can be bought at health food stores); however, the enema can be taken with plain water. For a do-it-yourself enema, 1 pint to 1 quart of water is sufficient.

The best position for taking an enema is on your knees, head down to the floor, with enema bag hanging 2½ to 3 feet above the anus, to get sufficient pressure in the flow of water. The flow can be regulated by squeezing the tube with the fingers; some enema bags have a special clamp to regulate the flow. Before inserting the nozzzle into the anus make sure there is no air left in the tube; let water run for a moment. Use some vaseline, oil or other lubricant on the nozzle to make insertion easier. If you feel discomfort or pain when water is running in, stop the flow for a while and take a few deep breaths; then continue again until the bag is empty.

If you can retain the water for a while and do not feel forced to empty the bowels at once, you may lie on a bed or soft rugs for a few minutes, and let the water do its dissolving and washing work before letting it out. First lie on the back for a minute, then on the right side, then on the stomach, and then on the left side. While you are doing this, gently massage your stomach with your hands. Then go to the toilet and let the water run out. Stay long enough to make sure that the bowels are empty.

The enema should be taken at least once each fasting day. The best time is the first thing in the morning. After the fast is broken, enemas should be continued until the bowels begin to move naturally without the help of the enemas. This usually takes two or three days. As soon as normal peristalsis is established, enemas should be discontinued.

Here are some additional points to watch:

- Make sure that the enema water is not too cold or too hot; it should be of body temperature, or slightly above.
- Keep the equipment clean; wash it with soap and water. If several people use the equipment, disinfect the nozzle with rubbing alcohol, then rinse with water.
- And, finally, watch for the copious amounts of debris and ill-smelling wastes coming out with the enema water, even after 5 weeks of fasting!

Note: the enemas are given in all European biological clinics that I am familiar with, and I am familiar with most of them. But the number of enemas varies with various practitioners. At Buchinger Sanatorium, enemas are given once every morning or every second morning. At Sweden's Björkagården Institute, as well as at Dr. Lars-

Erik Essén's Vita Nova (both presented in detail in my book, THERE IS A CURE FOR ARTHRITIS), enemas are administered 2 or 3 times a day — morning, noon and evening. Some clinics give enemas twice a day. My own recommendation is at least once a day, taken each morning.

CHAPTER 9

Detailed Program
For Do-It-Yourself
Juice Fasting

It is advisable to prepare yourself for fasting by a short cleansing diet. For 2 or 3 days eat nothing but raw fruits and vegetables — one meal a day of any vegetable fruits, the other of fresh vegetable salad.

Fasting usually begins with an effective bowel cleansing with the help of purgatives, such as Glauber's salts or castor oil. Dr. Buchinger uses an ounce and a half of Glauber's salts in one and a quarter pints of warm water on the morning of the first day of fasting. Since the Glauber's salt drink is not very tasty, it is usually followed by a glass of fruit juice. Glauber's salts will cause repeated and powerful evacuations and cleanse your bowels thoroughly. Some European clinics use castor oil for the same purpose. On the first day of fasting, one or two hours before an enema, two tablespoons of pure castor oil is taken in a glass of water to which the juice of half a lemon has been added. Of course, you can begin your fasting without purgative, just by taking a double enema. First take 1 pint of plain water and let it out. Then repeat with a full quart of water into which camomile tea or a few drops of lemon juice have been added.

The next day, and each following day of the fast, you follow this program:

UPON ARISING: Enema

AFTER ENEMA: Dry brush massage, followed by hot-and-cold shower. (See chapter 12 for instructions.)

9:00 A.M.:   Cup of herb tea — warm, not hot. Health food stores carry a large assortment of herb teas. I recommend a peppermint, camomile, or rose hips. See the instructions on the package for preparing the teas.

11:00 A.M.:   A glass of freshly-pressed fruit juice, diluted fifty-fifty with water.

11:00 A.M.
to 1:00 P.M.:   Walk or mild exercise, or sunbathing, if the weather permits. (In our Spa, various baths, massages and other treatments are given at this time.)

1:00 P.M.:   A glass of freshly made vegetable juice or a cup of vegetable broth*.

1:30 to 4:00 P.M.:   Rest in bed.

4:00 P.M.:   Cup of herb tea

4:15 to 7:00 P.M.:   Walk, therapeutic baths, exercises and other treatments.

7:00 P.M.:   Glass of diluted vegetable or fruit juices, or cup of vegetable broth.

Drink plain lukewarm water, or mineral water, when thirsty. The total juice and broth volume during the day should be between 1½ pints and 1½ quarts. Never dilute fresh juices with vegetable broth, only with pure water. The total liquid intake should be approximately 6 to 8 glasses — but don't hesitate to drink more, if thirsty.

Again, I suggest that, if at all possible, have your fasting supervised by someone who is well initiated in it. Under expert supervision such a fast could be undertaken at home up to 30 days, if necessary. If you suffer from some illness and are under your doctor's care, you may wish to

---

* See the next two chapters.

show this book and the fasting instructions to your own doctor and ask him to supervise your fasting and examine your condition as the fast progresses. Without expert supervision I would not advise fasting longer than one week to 10 days at a time. After a few weeks on a health-building diet (see Chapter 12) your fasting program may be repeated.

How the fast is broken

Whether your fast will turn out to be a success or a failure will depend largely on how you break your fast. **Breaking a fast is the most significant phase of it. The beneficial effect of fasting could be totally undone if the fast is broken incorrectly!** As Dr. Otto H. F. Buchinger says: "Even a fool can fast, but **only a wise man knows how to break the fast properly and to build up properly after the fast!**"

The main rules for breaking the fast are:

1. **Do not overeat!**

2. **Eat slowly and chew your food extremely well.**

3. **Take several days of gradual transition to the normal diet.**

First day:	Eat one whole apple in the morning and a very **small** bowl of raw vegetable salad at lunch, in addition to the usual juice and broth menu.
Second day:	Soaked prunes or figs (with the soaking water) for breakfast. Small bowl of fresh vegetable salad for lunch. Vegetable soup made without salt at dinner. Two apples eaten between meals. All this in addition to the usual juices and broths.
Third day:	As second day, but add a glass of yogurt and a few raw nuts for breakfast. Increase the salad portion at lunch, and add a boiled or baked potato. A slice of whole-grain bread with butter and a slice of cheese with soup at evening.

Fourth day: You may start eating normally, adhering to a cleansing macrobiotic diet*. If you fasted longer than 10 days, the break-in period should be extended one day for every 4 days of fasting.

In order to benefit from fasting to the greatest possible extent it is of paramount importance that after fasting a build-up diet of vital natural foods be maintained (See Chapter 12). Such a diet will supply the healing and regenerative forces of your body with all the needed elements, so that the cleansing, regenerative, rejuvenative and healing processes, initiated by the body during fasting, can be continued.

But **first and foremost,** keep always in mind the first rule of breaking the fast: **do not overeat!** This rule also happens to be the first rule of keeping healthy and staying younger longer.

---

* Outlined in detail in my book ARE YOU CONFUSED? Chapter 3.
See also THE AIROLA DIET & COOKBOOK.

CHAPTER 10

What Juices to Use For Specific Conditions

All juices used during fasting should be made fresh just before drinking. In fasting spas, various juices are prescribed individually, depending on the particular condition of the patient. For example, artihritics are not given citrus juices, except once or twice a week, the emphasis is instead on vegetable juices, particularly carrots, celery and alfalfa juices, and twice a day vegetable broths. In some other conditions, the emphasis is on fruit juices. Fruit and vegetable juices have a health-restorative, medicinal value and, prescribed individually, can be effectively used to speed the recovery.

If you are in a relatively healthy condition and are fasting for the purpose of purifying and cleansing your body and rejuvenating and regenerating all its vital functions, then you can use the juices of any available fruits and vegetables. Fruit juices most frequently used are: apple, orange, grapefruit, lemon, grapes, pineapple and pear In Mexican Spas, the juices of two tropical fruits, papaya and lima, are used frequently. The recommended vegetable juices are: carrot, celery, cabbage, red beets, and, of course, last but not least, the green juice, a "chlorophyll drink" made from green leaves of alfalfa, comfrey, carrot tops, beet tops, parsley, wheat grass, and/or any other available edible greens.

Here is a list of minerals, trace elements, vitamins, enzymes, coloring substances and other elements present in specific juices, with their prophylactic and therapeutic importance.*

Minerals in raw juices

CALCIUM: MDR** 0.8 gram. Present mostly in lemons, tangerines, elderberries, kale, mustard greens, carrots, kohlrabi, watercress, cabbage, and turnip and beet tops. Needed for bone formation, prevents inflammations and has a favorable preventive influence on tendency for hemorrhage. Involved in general metabolism.

POTASSIUM: MDR 0.5-1.0 g. Present in grapes, tangerines, lemons, parsley, spinach, potatoes, dandelions, celery, kale and most green leafy vegetables. Important for nerve and muscle function.

SODIUM: MDR 0.2-0.4 g. Present mostly in cherries, peaches, beets, dandelions, kale, carrots, celery, and tomatoes.

MAGNESIUM: MDR 0.3 g. Present mostly in elderberries, raspberries, lemons, endive and beets. Soothes nervous irritability, is important for muscle action and is indispensable in mineral and general metabolism.

PHOSPHORUS: MDR 0.9 g. Present in grapes, raspberries, tangerines, spinach, carrots, cabbage, beet tops, watercress and kale. Plays vital part in bone formation. Important for brain and nerve function.

* The following information is taken, in part, from the article RAW JUICES INSTEAD OF DRUGS, by Dr. Georg Lányi, M.D., published in TIDSKRIFT FÖR HÄLSA, June, 1967. Quoted with permission.
** Minimum Daily Requirement

SULPHUR: MDR 0.3 g. Present mostly in black and red currants, spinach, watercress and kale. Important in liver and skin-cell metabolism.

IRON: MDR 12 mg. Present in red and black currants, raspberries, spinach, apricots, parsley and beet tops. Vital for cell oxygenation as a constituent of hemoglobin.

Trace elements in raw juices

There is no exact information available in regard to the precise needs of these elements in human nutrition, but it has been established that deficiency in these substances can result in diseases in humans, animals and plants.

COPPER: Present in black and red currants, kale, potatoes and asparagus. Helps in iron absoption.

MANGANESE: Present in strawberries, apricots, oranges, green lettuce, spinach and kale. Involved, among other things, in reproductive processes.

ZINC: Present in apples, pears, kale, carrots, lettuce and asparagus. Needed for nerves. The healthy function of the prostate gland is dependent upon a sufficient amount of zinc in the diet.

COBALT: Present in apples, tomatoes, cabbage, carrots, beet tops, potatoes, and yellow onions. Assists in hemoglobin production.

FLUORINE: Present in black currants, cherries, spinach and carrots. In natural form, essential for bone and tooth formation.

IODINE: Present in oranges and spinach. Participates in metabolism through the thyroid gland.

SILICIC ACID: Present in strawberries, grapes, lettuce, string beans and carrots. Constitutes an important part of bone composition and is especially beneficial during healing processes.

Vitamins, enzymes, coloring substances, etc. in raw juices

Vitamin A: Does not occur in vitamin form in vegetables or fruits, but as a provitamin, **carotene,** which is transformed by the body into vitamin A. It is present mostly in carrots, spinach, tomatoes, green and red peppers, cabbage, celery, rose hips and oranges. Absorption of vitamin A into the digestive tract can be aided by the addition of linseed oil (flaxseed oil) or sesame seed oil to the juices.

Vitamin B_1: Present mostly in grapefruit, carrots, beets, beet tops, spinach and dandelion.

Vitamin B_2: Present mostly in parsley, turnip greens, carrots, beet tops, celery, green peppers, spinach and kale.

Vitamin B_3: Present mostly in parsley, kale, potatoes and asparagus.

Vitamin B_5: Present mostly in cabbage, cauliflower, strawberries, grapefruit and oranges.

Vitamin B_6: Present mostly in pears, spinach, potatoes, lemons and carrots.

Folic acid: Present mostly in spinach, parsley, carrots, potatoes and oranges.

Biotin: Present mostly in cauliflower, spinach, lettuce and grapefruit.

Inositol: Present mostly in oranges, grapefruit, cabbage, cauliflower, kale, beets, tomatoes, and onions.

Vitamin C:	The most known and universally used vitamin. The need is much greater than the tables usually recommend, especially during all kinds of stress and infections. Present in black currants, citrus fruits, green peppers, kale, cabbage, spinach, parsley and, most of all, in rose hips.
Vitamin K:	Present in spinach, cabbage and carrot tops.
Vitamin P:	Present mostly in grapes, oranges, black currants, rose hips, plums and green peppers.
Vitamin E:	Present in cold-pressed vegetable oils, especially in wheat germ oil.
Enzymes:	Many important enzymes are present in raw juices. Enzymes are made inactives by heating over 60 degrees C.
Coloring substances:	Yellow, red, green and blue coloring substances in all shades and intensities are present in large quantities in raw juices. They are vitally important from a therapeutic point of view. According to Dr. Georg Lányi, M.D., they increase production of red blood corpuscles, influence digestive and assimilative processes, and take part in the metabolism of proteins and cholesterol, etc.

In addition, raw juices contain the hormone-like substances, the "vegetable hormones," and antibiotic substances, which are, for example, present in garlic, onions, radishes, tomatoes, etc.

What diseases can be treated with raw juice therapy?

First it must be emphasized that every case is different and therefore all treatments must be adapted for every individual case. Especially with regard to fasting, the patient's physical and mental condition should be taken into consideration. It can vary from year to year in the same person! The suggestions given below are, therefore, to be considered only in a very general sense. If you suffer from a serious ailment it is best to consult a biologically-oriented doctor on the advisability of undertaking raw juice therapy. The following information should not be construed as **prescribing** for cases of illness, only as general information and a guide for the healing profession. Show the following pages to your doctor and ask him to advise and supervise your raw juice therapy.

Infectious diseases

The response to raw juice therapy in all forms of infectious disease is excellent. Tonsillitis also responds well.

The juices of black currants, lemons, oranges, pineapple, elderberries, beets, carrots, tomatoes, green peppers, watercress, onions, garlic (in very small doses), and rose hips are useful in the treatment of infectious diseases.

Stomach disorders

Gastric catarrh, or **gastritis,** responds well to the therapy of raw juices of carrots, tomatoes, celery, and potatoes. Cabbage juice (vitamin U) is considered specifically curative for gastric catarrh and stomach ulcers. **Liver and gall bladder** diseases **(gall bladder inflamation)** are best treated with the juice of grapes, carrots, and beets with small additions of juice from dandelions and radishes. Pear juice has been found very effective in the treatment of gall bladder diseases and gall stones. Diseases of the **small intestine** and all forms of constipation can be improved by raw juice therapy. Garlic exerts a cleansing effect on the bowels and is beneficial in cases of excessive gas. The juice of yellow onions has a similar, but milder, effect. These juices can be used in small amounts, one teaspoon or one tablespoon at a time. They may be mixed with milder vegetable juices, such as carrots, beets and celery.

For **chronic constipation** the following juices are recommended: spinach, watercress, garlic, yellow onions, black radish, and dandelion in addition to the milder juices of carrots, cucumber, tomatoes, red beets, and celery. Sauerkraut juice cleans bowels well, but some patients are troubled with gas when they use sauerkraut.

Of the fruit juices, apple and lemon are recommended in stomach disorders. Blueberries are excellent in cases of catarrhs; tea made from dried blueberries is the best medicine for diarrhea.

Blood and heart diseases

Variations in the amounts of red blood cells can be treated with juices. "Thick" blood, **polycythemia,** will be thinner after two or three weeks of juice therapy. The treatment can be repeated several times. For "thin" blood, **anemia,** spinach, kale and parsley juices are effective. They are rich in iron and chlorophyll, the green coloring matter of the leaves. These juices can be added to carrot juice in amounts of approximately three to four ounces a day. Also, grape juice is effective.

The dark colored juices of grapes, beets and blueberries help increase the production of red blood cells. Blood circulation is also improved by the juices, mainly because of the favorable strengthening effect they have on the tiny blood capillaries.

For disorders in the normal **heart function,** juices of hawthorn berries and garlic can be added to the other milder juices.

Blood pressure

The best thing to do for **high blood pressure** is to go on a juice fast. Juices supply blood and tissues with the important mineral, potassium, which helps to eliminate accumulated sodium chloride (salt) from the tissues. A juice fast for high blood pressure should be of three to four weeks duration. Usually in this period of time the blood pressure goes down to normal. This therapy can be repeated several times with an interval of six months between each fast. The most suitable juices for high blood pressure are citrus fruits, black currants and grapes, plus carrots, spinach, beets, parsley, onions and garlic (as an addition). Even in **low blood pressure** a juice fast can be tried, preferably under a doctor's supervision. In this case the useful juices are pineapple, celery, black radish, onion and garlic in addition to carrot, red beet and grape juice.

For **edema,** or water-logged body tissues, juices of pears and dandelions are used.

Leg ulcers

Leg ulcers heal faster with raw juice therapy. Juices of onion and garlic are added to carrot juice. Also effective are citrus and apple juices. A dressing of cabbage or comfrey leaves and yellow onions over the ulcer speeds the healing process.

Obesity

Raw juice fasting is obviously a very appropriate therapy for **obesity.** Juices of celery, watercress, parsley, lemon, grapefruit, pineapple and grape juice are specifically valuable. The duration of treatment is three to four weeks, or even much longer if necessary.

Rheumatic diseases

Rheumatic diseases are particularly responsive to juice therapy. Fasts of four to six weeks can be recommended. The alkaline action of raw juices dissolves the accumulation of deposits around the joints. The combination of other biological therapies is advisable — massage, hydrotherapy, etc. In cases of **gout,** a noticeable worsening of the condition may develop in the early stages of fasting when uric acid, dissolved by juices, is thrown into the blood stream for elimination. In very advanced cases it is difficult to bring about a permanent improvement, but juice fasting always causes a definite improvement in the condition. Serious **arthritic** deformities of long standing cannot be corrected, of course, but the function of the deformed joints can be greatly improved. Juices most valuable in these situations are carrot, beet, parsley, alfalfa, potatoes and celery. Even juices rich in vitamin C can be used, but citrus juices only sparingly. Rheumatic diseases are collagen diseases and vitamin C is essential for healthy collagen. Also, daily use of vegetable broth (see recipe in the next chapter) is advisable, as one of the characteristics of rheumatic diseases is a mineral imbalance in the tissues, and particularly the lack of potassium. Vegetable broth is rich in potassium and other minerals.

Diabetes

Even **diabetics** can try juice therapy, **but only under a sympathetic doctor's control.** The carbohydrate content of juices is not high; besides, a certain amount of carbohydrate is good for diabetics. (Fat is burned in the "fire" of the carbohydrates!) The leg ulcers of diabetics heal faster during juice therapy. Young diabetics should engage in strenuous sports; heavy physical work and exertion diminish the need for insulin.

Juices for the treatment of diabetes are: string beans, parsley, cucumber, celery, watercress, lettuce, onions, garlic and citrus juices. Cucumber contains a hormone needed by the cells of the pancreas in order to produce insulin. The hormones contained in onions are also beneficial in diabetes. **Note:** string bean skin tea is considered by many biological doctors to be a natural substitute for insulin and extremely beneficial in diabetes. The skins of the pods of green beans are very rich in silicic acid and certain hormonal substances which are closely related to insulin. One cup of bean skin tea is equal to at least one unit of insulin. The recommended dose: one cup of string bean skin tea morning, noon and evening (Waerland).

Kidney disorders

Kidney diseases and **prostate disorders** can be coped with successfully using raw juices. The juice of horse radish (small amount), watercress and birch leaves can be added to carrot and celery juice. Lemon juice is effective in dissolving uric acid stones in the bladder. For prostate disorders, pumpkin juice is reported to be specifically beneficial.

Skin diseases

Various forms of **eczema** and other skin eruptions have been successfully treated for years with fasting methods. A certain worsening of the condition can be expected in the beginning, due to the increased elimination of waste matter. The colorful juices of black currants, red grapes, carrots, beets and spinach are recommended. Cucumber juice, internally and externally, is specifically advised for the treatment of skin diseases; it possesses acknowledged cosmetic properties.

Nervousness and Insomnia

Recommended juices for conditions of nervousness and insomnia are apples, carrots, oranges and celery.

Emphysema

The raw juice of carrots, parsnip, watercress and potatoes is beneficial (Dr. N. W. Walker). Of fruits, the juice of oranges, lemons, black currants and rose hips (as tea).

Goiter

Goiter, or enlargement of the thyroid gland due to iodine deficiency, can be treated with the juice of carrots, parsley, spinach, celery and a special vegetable broth (see recipe in next chapter), to which 1 tsp. of powdered kelp has been added during cooking. Kelp, sea lettuce, dulce, or other seaweed, are the best natural source of organic iodine.

Halitosis, or bad breath

Green, chlorophyll-rich juices of parsley, spinach, watercress, lettuce, alfalfa, and beet tops combined with carrots and celery, are excellent for treating halitosis caused by the retention of toxic waste water in the tissues. Two glasses of vegetable broth a day is also advisable.

Asthma

The best juices for asthma are: lemon, lime, horse radish and garlic. Garlic and horse radish juices can be taken in small amounts mixed with the juices of carrots and red beets. Lemon juices can be taken diluted with water first thing in the morning. Asthma patients can also take lemon juice **plain,** one teaspoonful 2-3 times a day.

Do-it-yourself raw juice treatment

In the limited space of one chapter it would be impossible to give all the facts and answers related to the vast and complicated subject of raw juice therapy. I hope, however, that this presentation will serve as a stimulus to use raw juices, this time-proven biological remedy, in the treatment of many disorders where orthodox medical treatments are helpless.

In the case of serious conditions, such as diabetes, low blood pressure, acute conditions and serious infections, it would be advisable to undertake raw juice therapy under expert professional control.

In chronic and less serious conditions, and particularly when used as a prophylactic measure, raw juice therapy can be safely undertaken on your own. The most effective therapeutic way to use raw juices is in conjunction with fasting. Follow the instructions given in this book carefully, especially the instruction regarding the breaking of the fast.

In addition to their pure medicinal property in the treatment of practically any disease, raw juices have an extraordinary revitalizing effect on all the organs of the body. The miraculous rejuvenative property of a raw juice diet is well known by all beauty farms and rejuvenating clinics, where raw juices are used extensively. The magic beautifying, "youthifying" and rejuvenating effect of raw juices is due to their cleansing and detoxifying property. Raw juices purify the blood and all the tissues of the body, neutralize the waste products of metabolism, and help in building new tissues. They are indeed rightfully called "the internal bath of health and youth."

PRACTICAL POINTS TO REMEMBER

1. All raw juices should be freshly prepared.
2. Use an electric juice extractor. The large department stores carry various types. Follow the instruction booklet that comes with the juicer.
3. Use only fresh vegetables and fruits, preferably organically grown (available at better health food stores and organic farms). If vegetables and fruits are bought from the ordinary supermarket they have probably been heavily sprayed with poisonous insecticides and waxes. Wash them carefully. I use warm water and soap or a mild detergent to wash such vegetables and fruits as apples, pears, grapes, plums, cucumbers, carrots, green peppers, tomatoes and celery. Rinse well, three or four times in progressively colder water. Give the final rinse under running water, rubbing vigorously with a brush and with your hands.
4. Make only as much juice as needed. In storage, even in the refrigerator, raw juices rapidly lose their therapeutic and nutritional value.

CHAPTER II

The Importance of
Vegetable Broth

Vegetable broth is one of the standard beverages during fasting in all biological clinics in Europe. Fasting patients at our Spa receive a large glass of vegetable broth first thing in the morning and before going to bed. It is a cleansing and alkalizing drink which supplies a great amount of vitamins and particularly minerals, which are so important for establishing and normalizing a proper chemical balance in the tissues during fasting. Vegetable broth is particularly rich in the mineral potassium. For this reason, some people call it "potassium broth". Potassium is of special importance in the treatment of rheumatic diseases and arthritis. Here's how you make it:

Vegetable broth

2 large potatoes, unpeeled, chopped or sliced to approximately one-half-inch pieces.
1 cup carrots, shredded or sliced
1 cup red beets, shredded or sliced
1 cup celery, leaves and all, chopped to one-half-inch pieces

1 cup any other available vegetables: beet tops, turnips and turnip tops, parsley, cabbage or a little of everything. However, a satisfactory broth can be made with only potatoes, beets, carrots, and celery, consisting of approximately 50% potatoes, 20% carrots, 15% beets and 15% celery.

Use stainless steel, enameled or earthenware utensil. Fill it up with one and one-half quarts of water and slice the vegetables directly into the water to prevent oxidation. Do not peel potatoes, beets or carrots, just brush them well. Cover and cook slowly for at least a half hour. Let stand for another half hour; strain, cool until warm and serve. If not used immediately, keep in refrigerator. Warm it up before serving.

"Excelsior"

"Excelsior" drink is a variation of vegetable broth especially for patients with constipation problems and those with stomach and bowel disorders. Flax seeds have a healing effect on the stomach and bowel linings as well as act as a natural, mild laxative. Bran supplies necessary bulk and stimulates normal peristalsis. "Excelsior" should be used after fasting at least for the first few days or weeks, until the normal peristaltic rhythm is established.

    1 cup of vegetable broth as above
    1 tbsp. whole flaxseed
    1 tbsp. raw wheat bran

Flaxseed and wheat bran can be bought at health food stores. Soak flaxseed and wheat bran in vegetable broth overnight. In the morning, stir well, warm up and drink — seeds and all. Do not chew the flaxseeds, drink them whole. Actually, it would be better not to **drink** excelsior, but **eat** it slowly with a spoon, but without chewing, to effect proper salivation.

CHAPTER 12

More Tips On Juice Fasting

Can you work while fasting?

Should you discontinue with your work and rest or stay in bed while fasting? Not at all! On the contrary, staying in bed while fasting is definitely harmful. Your body needs lots of assistance in the form of fresh air, motion and exercise, in order to accomplish a thorough cleansing of the blood and tissues and to effectively regenerate and revitalize all the body functions. Therefore, patients in the fasting clinics are advised to do lots of walking and mild exercises, especially deep breathing exercises, in addition to sunbathing. If you fast on your own, it is advisable to continue with your normal activities, but perhaps avoid **too** strenuous physical or mental work. But do not neglect your daily walks. Do deep breathing exercises while you walk.

Daily baths

It is generally believed that one-third of all body impurities and wastes are eliminated through the skin. Since the tissue cleansing and speedy elimination of toxic wastes is a prime purpose of fasting, it is important to keep the skin pores wide open and the elimination through the skin as efficient as possible. Daily showers, especially in conjunction with dry brush massage are recommended. If the heart and circulation are good (your doctor must determine this) then hot baths, steambaths (sauna) and hot-and-cold showers should be taken frequently. (See chapter on Therapeutic Baths in my book, HOW TO GET WELL.)

The importance of dry brush massage

During fasting — in fact, during the whole period of biological treatment — all our patients are advised to take dry brush massage. This is a simple and easy method of rejuvenating and revitalizing your skin and of increasing its eliminative capacity.

Dry brush massage is taken for about 10 to 15 minutes each morning before the hot-and-cold shower, and again before going to bed at night.

Here's how you take dry brush massage. Get a natural bristle brush with a long handle (available at most health food stores — if not, you may use a regular vegetable brush that you can get at any drug or hardware store. Warning: Do not use nylon or synthetic fibre brushes — they are too sharp and may damage the skin). Starting with the soles of your feet, brush vigorously, making rotary motions, and massage every part of your body. Brush in this order: first feet and legs, then hands and arms, then back and abdomen, chest and neck. Brush until your skin becomes rosy, warm and glowing. Five to fifteen minutes is the average time.

The best time for brush massage is upon arising in the morning, and again before going to bed at night. After dry brush massage it is advisable to take a shower or a rubdown with a sponge or wet towel to wash away dead skin particles loosened by the brushing.

Your skin is your largest eliminative organ. Hundreds of thousands of tiny sweat glands act not only as the regulators of body temperature, but also as small kidneys, the detoxifying organs which are ready to cleanse the blood and free the system from health-threatening poisons. If the skin becomes inactive and its pores choked with millions of dead cells then the uric acid and other impurities, that are normally excreted through the skin, will remain in your body, overworking the kidneys and poisoning the whole system.

In addition to its eliminative work, skin has many other vital functions. Your body actually breathes through the skin, absorbing oxygen and exhaling carbon dioxide. Also, through the skin certain nutrients are absorbed into the body. Scientists have demonstrated that most nutrients, such as vitamins, minerals, oils and even proteins can be assimilated into the system when applied directly to the skin. Vitamin D is produced directly on the skin by the action of sun rays and consequently absorbed into the body.

As you can see, your skin is a living, vital organ with multiplicity of important functions. The tragedy is that it is the most mistreated organ of modern man, who but seldom exposes his skin to the elements of nature, to perspiration and to other stimulation.

Here is an impressive list of benefits you derive from regularly performed dry brush massage:

- It will effectively remove the dead layers of skin and other impurities, and keep pores open.
- It will stimulate and increase blood circulation all over the body.
- It will stimulate hormone and oil-producing glands.
- It has a powerful rejuvenating influence on the nervous system by stimulating nerve endings in the skin.
- It will help to prevent colds, especially when used in combination with hot-and-cold showers.
- It will rejuvenate the complexion and make it look younger, fresher and more velvety.

Dry brush massage should be taken by all sincere health seekers all the time, but is of particular importance during fasting, when the body is cleansing itself of toxins.

Read more about dry brush massage in my book ARE YOU CONFUSED?, in the Chapter titled **"Dry brush massage — a million dollar health and beauty secret."**

What teas to drink during fasting

As you can see from the program of do-it-yourself fasting in Chapter 9, I advocate drinking herb teas once or twice a day.

I am always asked what teas are the best? This question is not easy to answer, although I have my favorites. For the best effect, herb teas should be prescribed by the doctor. In Europe, it is possible to buy at drugstores or health food stores hundreds of various herbs which are specifically recommended for various conditions. There are also available special herb combinations as specifics for arthritis, heart disease, diabetes, digestive disorders, liver, kidneys, etc. But in the United States, the FDA would not allow labeling herbs as having any medicinal value; therefore, the herbs, although available in a great variety in health food stores, are not labeled as to what condition they are recommended for. Thus the customer is left in the dark — or he must study the professional herb manuals to find out which herbs are good for what condition.

Medicinal value of herbs is well documented, and books are available on their proper use. It would be impossible to go into detail on the medicinal property of each herb in this book. Get some good herb books and study them — then use the herbs that are specifically beneficial for your condition.

One of the best herbs with the broadest range of usefulness is **peppermint.** It has a calming and strengthening effect on the nerves and has been used for ages as a home remedy for gas, indigestion, nausea and flatulence. It also has a mild antiseptic property.

Another of my favorites is **camomile.** It is useful in colds, throat infections, catarrhal conditions and digestive problems. A cup of camomile tea before going to bed will help to get a good night of sleep. Because of its antitoxic property, it is useful as an additive to the enema water (one cup of tea to a quart of water).

Rose hip tea is an excellent tea to take during fasting. It is an extremely rich source of vitamin C and bioflavonoids (vitamin C-complex). It will help to speed up the healing activity during fasting. Vitamin C is also a **number one** beauty secret* — it helps to keep collagen elastic and strong. Vitamin C deficient collagen is mostly responsible for the early appearance of wrinkles.

For those who fast primarily for the purpose of rejuvenation, the old favorites **ginseng, fo-ti-tieng, gotu kola** and **sarsaparilla** can be tried. They all have been used for centuries in various parts of the world as the secrets of perpetual youth. Ginseng and fo-ti-tieng have strengthening and revitalizing effect on brain, nerve and glandular functions. They help to revitalize the activity of sex glands — and diminished hormone production of sex glands is considered to be one of the main causes of premature aging and senility. Sarsaparilla is a known aphrodisiac, which contains sex hormones **testosterone** and **progesterone.** It also contains the adrenal hormone **cortin.**

Your favorite health food store has a good supply of herb teas, those mentioned above as well as many others.

Should you drink water — and what kind

The juice fasting program as suggested in this book gives you 5 glasses of juices, broths and herb teas during 24 hours. If you feel thirsty, you may drink 2-3 additional glasses of water. It depends much on the climate and the time of the year you do your fasting. If it is a hot summer and you perspire a lot and do lots of exercises and walks, you need more liquids than if you fast during the winter time.

The best water to drink is natural, pure, unpolluted spring or well water. Avoid chlorinated or fluoridated water. I do not advise drinking distilled water. Distilled water is a man-made, processed, artifical, fragmented product. Contrary to what some "experts" advise, the minerals in the natural "hard" water do **not** cause hardening of the arteries or other alleged diseases. It has been established that where drinking water is extremely hard, i.e. it contains extra large amounts of minerals and trace elements, the people have a much lower incidence of arteriosclerosis and caries, as compared to the areas where

---

* SWEDISH BEAUTY SECRETS, Chapter One.

people drink so-called soft water. Inorganic minerals and trace elements in water have important functions in the metabolic processes of your body. They act as catalysts and stimulants, and are extremely beneficial. Recent research shows that your body can assimilate minerals through the skin from sea air or sea water. Mineral waters in bathing spas around the world have been used for health-restoring purposes for thousands of years. If you can get natural mineral water, take one glass of it each day. One tablespoon of pure sea water in a glass of regular water can also be taken each day. (See an interesting and illuminating chapter called **Water Controversies** in my book ARE YOU CONFUSED?)

Health-building diet after the fast

Whether you fast for reducing, healing or rejuvenating purposes, the diet **after** the fast is of utmost importance. The regenerative, rejuvenative and healing processes initiated by your body during fasting must continue **after** the fast is broken. Most of the wonderful results achieved during fasting will be nullified in a very short time if fasting is followed by the diet that created the undesirable condition in the first place — a condition that fasting corrected so successfully.

The best health-building diet, or the diet with the greatest potential for optimum health, long life and prevention of disease, is, what I call, the **modern macrobiotic diet,** described in detail in my book ARE YOU CONFUSED?

The basic rules of a health-building diet are:

1. **You should eat only NATURAL foods.** Natural foods are foods that are grown in fertile soils without chemicals, and are unprocessed, unadulterated, and untampered with. Pasteurized milk, canned foods, chemicalized and processed foods can not sustain health, but will bring disease and premature aging.

2. **You should eat only WHOLE foods.** Whole foods are simply foods which contain all the nutrients nature has put into them. Whole wheat, potatoes in jackets, brown rice,

sugar cane — are whole foods. White bread, instant potatoes, polished rice, white sugar and orange juice are not whole foods. They are refined, fragmented and adulterated. White bread is the classic example of adulterated food, from which most of the health-building elements have been removed or destroyed. The fact that it is "fortified" makes it, if anything, even worse: adding four synthetic nutrients, after removing or processing out over 20 natural nutrients, can only cause a dangerous nutritive imbalance in your body. Fragmented, refined and processed foods can invariably lead to disease and premature aging. They are also one of the main causes of obesity; no matter how much you eat of them, you still feel hungry because your body is not getting the nutrients it needs!

3. **You should eat only LIVING** foods. Cooking destroys enzymes 100%. Enzymes are vital catalysts, absolutely essential for the proper digestion and assimilation of food, as well as for all other functions of your body. It has been shown that you need only half of the amount of protein if it is eaten in the raw form. Cooking also destroys many vitamins and makes minerals, proteins and fats less assimilable.

Raw foods have a definite therapeutic value. Only living foods can build healthy bodies and prevent disease and premature aging. At least 75% of all the foods you eat should be in a natural raw state.

4. **Eat only POISON-FREE foods.** Poisons in foods are the greatest menace to health today. Make an effort to either grow most of your own food or buy organically grown and produced foods obtainable at most health food stores.

5. **Eat high natural carbohydrates—low animal protein diet.** Contrary to what you have been reading and learning from America's most respected nutritional advisors and health "experts", a **HIGH PROTEIN DIET IS DEFINITELY HARMFUL!** It is too long a story to go into detail here — get my book ARE YOU CONFUSED? where I discuss this subject in detail and **prove conclusively** that it is not the **high protein**—low carbohydrate diet, but the

high natural carbohydrate—low animal protein diet that has the greatest potential for optimal health, maximum vitality and long life. Modern scientific research, as well as empirical experience proves this conclusively. Too much protein in your diet can cause accumulation of uric acid, urea and toxic purines in the tissues; biochemical imbalance in the tissues and resultant overacidity; intestinal putrefaction, constipation and auto-toxemia; vitamin B_6 deficiency; arteriosclerosis, heart disease and kidney damage; it is also one of the contributing causes of arthritis. A high animal protein diet is **one** of the main causes of why American health is at such a low level as compared to most other civilized countries.

Mark well, I recommend a high **natural** carbohydrate diet, not **refined** carbohydrates. Natural carbohydrates are: whole grains, nuts, seeds, vegetables and fruits, potatoes, bananas, etc. It has been scientifically established that raw vegetable proteins, as found, for example in potatoes, green vegetables, and almonds, are biologically, **much superior** to proteins in meat. The best health-building diet is a so-called lacto-vegetarian diet with emphasis on whole grains (barley, oats, millet, sesame and rice are especially beneficial), seeds, nuts, fruits and vegetables, supplemented with milk and milk products, vegetable oil and honey.

Incidentally, those who found it difficult to eliminate meat from their diet have discovered that fasting is the best way to get rid of the desire for meat. Excessive meat eating, because of the toxic uric acid and purine content of the meat, is habit forming — just like smoking, coffee drinking or salt eating are. During fasting much of the uric acid accumulation in the system is excreted and, consequently, all the desire for meat eating will gradually disappear.

6. **Learn the correct, health-promoting eating habits.** Finally, not only **what** you eat, but **how** you eat and **how much** you eat is of paramount importance to your health. The latest scientific research shows that **systematic overeating** is one of the main causes of most of man's ills, and

that, conversely, **systematic undereating** is singularly the most important health and longevity factor. Russian centenarians are **all** moderate eaters. Dr. C.M. McCay's experiments at Cornell University demonstrated that overeating is the major cause of premature aging. Undereating, on the other hand, increases longevity and sharply decreases the incidence of the degenerative diseases. Food eaten in excess of the actual body needs acts in the system as a poison.

Slow eating and good mastication are essential for good health. Never eat in a hurry. Never eat when not really hungry. Always eat in a relaxed atmosphere — and **enjoy** what you eat. Biologically, only the foods eaten with genuine pleasure will do you any good.

Follow the above six rules of macrobiotic eating for optimum health after your fasting and you will be building upon — not tearing down — the good results the fasting has accomplished.

Contraindications for fasting

There are a few conditions where prolonged fasting is not advised, such as advanced cases of tuberculosis, active malignancies, advanced diabetes, during pregnancy or lactation, and in extreme emaciation. Extremely emaciated patients should not fast longer than three days at a time, with intervals of a nourishing diet. Where there is serious, acute disease, do not attempt fasting without consulting your doctor and abiding by his decision on the advisability of undertaking a fast.

Drugs and fasting

As a rule, a **complete withdrawal** of all drugs is advised during a fast. However, in certain conditions when drugs have been used for a long time and a certain body dependence has built up, *withdrawal of drugs should be gradual and the effect of withdrawal carefully supervised by a doctor.* Insulin in diabetes, digitalis in heart disease, or cortisone in arthritis or other diseases — and a few other drugs — should never be withdrawn suddenly and completely, but gradually, by diminishing the dosage each day. This even applies to regular coffee, if the patient has, for example, a heart condition and has been a heavy coffee-addict for years.

Should you take vitamins while fasting?

I am positively an advocate of taking vitamins and food supplements — for the healthly as well as for the sick — mainly because of our devitalized foods and toxic environment. Also, I use vitamins extensively, often in huge doses, in my therapeutic nutritional programs for practically any condition of ill health. But while fasting, the intake of vitamins or other food supplements should be discontinued completely. The general rule is that vitamin and mineral supplements should be taken only when food is eaten; they can be properly used by the body only in combination with foods.

However, as with drugs in certain conditions, there are cases when vitamins can be allowed while fasting. Serious heart cases, for example, are given vitamin E during the fast, although in diminished dosage. The doctor who supervises your fast must determine the necessity of continuing with vitamins while fasting.

As soon as the fast is broken, from the second or third day, the usual vitamin supplementation can be resumed.

Smoking and fasting

I have been asked: "Can I smoke while fasting?" The answer is: Of course not! It is indeed unwise to try to build up your health and tear it down at the same time. Smoking will harm you even more during the fasting, when your body needs all the possible fresh air and oxygen it can get.

Incidentally, fasting is the **best** way to quit smoking for good. After about two weeks of fasting all the desire for smoking will be gone. I have known many habitual smokers who were able to quit smoking through fasting.

Will you feel hungry during fasting?

Yes, during the first three or four days you will feel hungry, of course. But after that the hunger usually disappears. As a matter of fact, the unbelievable will happen: the longer you fast the less hungry you feel. Finally, when the body has completed its cleansing and restorative work it will signal by a sudden and definite feeling of hunger that you should start eating. This is physiologically the right time to break the fast. Of course, in the case of juice fasts, even during the first three or four days you will hardly feel any hunger at all. However, every patient reacts differently in this respect; much of it depends on the mental attitude. Those who are not totally convinced of the positive properties of fasting, or if they fast unwillingly (nobody should fast unwillingly!), they will feel more hungry than those who have complete faith and confidence in fasting. The amount of will power and determination plays an important role, too. Some of the fasting patients come to our dining room, where a smorgasbord loaded with most appetizing dishes tempts them, and drink their water or juice without being tempted in the least. Others beg every day to let them start eating, although all symptoms indicate they have no real physiological appetite. This difference in the personality makeup is one good reason why the best way to fast is at a fasting clinic or health Spa where the practitioner can closely observe the patient, encourage him to continue, and explain his various reactions and symptoms, and where fasting guests encourage one another.

The importance of positive mental attitude

Mental attitude during fasting is of paramount importance. Avoid negative influences. Do not listen to terrified relatives and "friends" who will warn you that you will pass out any moment. As I said before, nobody has ever died as a result of a few weeks of intentional fasting. Have confidence in what you are doing. Remember, you are not the first to try it — millions of people have done it successfully before you. If it makes you feel better, do not call this measure a fast, call it a Juice diet.

It is best not to tell your friends of your new exciting venture until the fast is completed. If they know you are fasting, they will study you carefully and tell you how much worse you look each day. If they don't know of your fasting, they will ask you, "What's happening? You look better and better each day!" Such is human nature! I know from a quarter of a century of experience that when your fast is over, both you and your friends will be surprised and amazed at the remarkable — yes, miraculous — transformation that has taken place.

Fasting and spiritual awareness

Fasting not only accomplishes a physiological regeneration and revitalization of your body, but has a profound stimulating effect on your mental faculties. It also increases your spiritual awareness. It is important, therefore, to adopt a proper relaxed attitude. Try to dissociate yourself from the usual everyday problems and the worries of the material world, and let the refinement and perfection of your inner self come to the fore as the ultimate purpose of your existence.

Fasting is the time of rest, meditation and renewal of body, mind and spirit. In most religions — Oriental, Hebrew, Christian, Muhammadan — periodic fasting played a vital part, for two reasons: **one,** to keep the body (the temple of the spirit) clean; **two,** to keep the spirit attuned with its Divine source.

You will notice that during fasting your visual and mental perception and awareness of aesthetic beauty will be sharpened and that your thoughts will gradually raise from a lower, everyday level of unpleasant realities to higher realities, concerned with the purpose and meaning of your Divinely designed life. Your daily walk in the woods will be a new and totally different experience. The singing of the birds will sound like the most inspiring Bach-oratory, and the tall trees will appear as mystic gothic cathedrals. Your heart will rejoice, your earthly problems will seem unimportant, and you'll feel happy to be alive. You will count your blessings instead of your problems. And you will be amazed at how your mental activity will be sharpened and how thoughts and new ideas will flow with ease.

All in all, your first fasting will be a wonderful experience, which will recharge, renew and rejuvenate your whole personality — body, mind and spirit!

BIBLIOGRAPHY

Buchinger, Otto H.F., ABOUT FASTING, Thorsons Publishers, Ltd. London, 1966

Buchinger, Otto H.F., HEILFASTENKUR, Bruno Wilkens, Verlag, Hannover

Waerland, Are and Ebba, HEALTH IS YOUR BIRTHRIGHT, Humata Publishers, Bern, Switzerland

Berg, Ragnar, WHY WE DIE, Nordiska Bookhandelns Förlag, Stockholm, 1947

Zabel, W., DAS FASTEN, Hippokrates Verlag, Giessen-Stuttgart, 1951

Lànyi, Georg, RAW JUICES INSTEAD OF DRUGS, Tidskrift För Hälsa, June 1967, Stockholm, Sweden

Walker, N.W., RAW VEGETABLE JUICES, Norwalk Press, Publishers, Phoenix, Arizona, 1936

Airola, Paavo O., ARE YOU CONFUSED?, Health Plus, Publishers, Sherwood, Oregon, 1970

Airola, Paavo O., HEALTH SECRETS FROM EUROPE, Parker Publishing Co., Inc., West Nyack, N.Y., 1970

DeVries, Arnold, THERAPEUTIC FASTING, Chandler Book Co., Los Angeles, Calif., 1963

Selye, Hans, THE STRESS OF LIFE, McGraw-Hill Book Co., Inc., New York

Buchinger, Otto, HEILUNG DER MANDELENTZÜNDUNG, Bruno Wilkens Verlag, Hannover, 1960

Buchinger, Otto, RETREAT, Turm Verlag Bietigheim/Württ, 1967

Bircher, Ruth, EATING YOUR WAY TO HEALTH, Faber and Faber, London, 1961

Bircher-Benner, WAY TO POSITIVE HEALTH, Bircher-Benner Verlag, Erlenback-Zürich, 1967

Warmbrand, Max, THE ENCYCLOPEDIA OF NATURAL HEALTH, Groton Press, New York

Carrington, Hereward, FASTING FOR HEALTH AND LONG LIFE, Health Research, Mokelumne Hill, California, 1963

Vogel, Alfred, THE NATURE DOCTOR, Bioforce-Verlag, Teufen, Switzerland, 1960

ABOUT THE AUTHOR

Paavo Airola, Ph.D., N.D., is an internationally-recognized nutritionist, naturopathic physician, educator, and award-winning author. Raised and educated in Europe, he studied biochemistry, nutrition, and natural healing in biological medical centers of Sweden, Germany, and Switzerland. He lectured extensively world-wide, both to professionals and laymen, holding yearly educational seminars for physicians. He has been a visiting lecturer at many universities and medical schools, including the Stanford University Medical School.

Dr. Paavo Airola is the author of fourteen widely-read books, notably his two international best-sellers, *How to Get Well*, and *Are You Confused? How to Get Well* is the most authoritative and practical manual on natural healing in print. It is used as a textbook in several universities and medical schools, and regarded as a reliable reference manual, the "Bible of Natural Healing," by doctors, researchers, nutritionists, and students of health and holistic healing. Dr. Airola's book, *Hypoglycemia: A Better Approach*, has revolutionized the therapeutic concept of this insidious, complex, and devastating affliction. The American Academy of Public Affairs issued Dr. Airola the Award of Merit for his book on arthritis.

Dr. Airola's monumental work, *Everywoman's Book*, is a great new contribution in the field of holistic medicine. It not only confirms Dr. Airola's unchallenged leadership in the field of nutrition and holistic healing, but demonstrates his genius as an original thinker, philosopher, and profound humanitarian.

The Airola Diet & Cookbook is Dr. Airola's newest book. It contains not only 300 delicious and nutritious recipes and Dr. Airola's Weight Loss Program, but also the most thorough presentation to date of the scientific basis for the Airola Optimum Diet — the world-famous diet of supernutrition for superhealth.

Dr. Airola is President of the International Academy of Biological Medicine; a member of the International Naturopathic Association; and a member of the International Society for Research on Civilization Diseases and Environment, the prestigious Forum for world-wide research founded by Dr. Albert Schweitzer. Dr. Airola is listed in the *Directory of International Biography, The Blue Book, The Men of Achievement, Who's Who in American Art, Who's Who in the West,* and *Canadian Who's Who.*